The Making of a Minor Poet

GW00497112

Selected Poems

by

Randle Manwaring

Published by Feather Books
PO Box 438
Shrewsbury SY3 0WN, UK
Tel/fax; 01743 872177

Website URL: http://www.waddysweb.freeuk.com
e-mail: john@waddysweb.freeuk.com

Dedication

To John Pearce M.A. (Oxon),
Prebendary St Paul's Cathedral, London 1970-1977.
My Kinsman in the Faith and in Poetry

Printed and bound in Great Britain by
4edge Ltd, Hockley. www.4edge.co.uk

ISBN: 978-1-84175-252-5

No. 262 in the Feather Books Poetry Series

Preface

In compiling my "SELECTED" I asked three of my long-standing friends – all knowledgeable on poetry, but (apart from a married couple), not knowing each other, to help me choose the appropriate poems for this volume. I am indebted to them for their help and I would like to mention their names:

Professor Gwilym Evans and his wife Angela

and Prebendary John Pearce

Many of the earliest poems chosen are ones which I wrote when I was 18 or 19 and these are included to show, as I hoped, the beginnings of development in craft and poetic sensitivity. I think this may have been achieved.

R.M. 2006

The Making of a Minor Poet

William Wordsworth declared that poetry is *the spontaneous overflow of powerful feeling: it takes its origin from emotion recollected in tranquillity* and I therefore feel grateful that I have been blessed with a retentive memory which sometimes awakens thoughts for a new poem. Also, I inherited from my father an ability with words. In his daily working life, he was one of the two Assistant Librarians of the London Library and met many of the leading authors of his day, notably Rudyard Kipling, John Masefield, Henry Newbolt and Walter de la Mare. In addition, my father found time to write books of naval history, being regarded as the leading authority on the Nelson period and he wrote, with Professor Bonamy Dobrée, who later held the chair of English at Leeds University, *The Floating Republic*, an account of the Naval Mutinies. Altogether my father wrote or edited about a dozen books of this kind.

My aunt, Helen Manwaring, supervised the return of books at the Library and got to know, in her quiet, unobtrusive way, men like Masefield and Kipling. (Masefield, the poet laureate, never failed to send her some of his verses for Christmas).

Not surprisingly, the staff at the library were allowed to borrow any books they fancied and I was therefore delighted when my aunt brought home for me books of poems. These supplemented the books on our shelves at home, notably, as I remember, the poetry of Henry Longfellow and Alfred Tennyson: Their ballad style poetry had much in common and I recall reciting it to myself when I was, I suppose, about ten or eleven. *Hiawatha* and *The Charge of the Light Brigade* became firm favourites and I liked to stand at the top of the stairs to recite or read.

But it was not until study for the Cambridge Junior and Senior examinations, when I was a young teenager that poetry, as I believe, took hold of my soul when *An Anthology of Modern Verse* became part of me. By 1926, Methuen had published 21 editions, including many specially for schools. It was dedicated '*To Thomas Hardy, OM, greatest of the moderns*' with a substantial introduction by Robert Lynd and appropriately carried on its flyleaf the words of Matthew Arnold – '*By nothing is England so glorious as by her poetry*'. The Anthology included the poems of about 100 poets, all famous or thereabouts in their day; Hardy was close to the end of his very distinguished literary life and Eliot, near the beginning of his, was in his thirties. Many of the poets belonged to what was known as the Georgian group, including lesser lights such as John Drinkwater, J. C. Squire and the more famous Edmund Blunden. Outstandingly there were the war poets, from the glamorous Rupert Brooke to those killed in action such as Wilfred Owen and Julian Grenfell. There were also and very significantly those who lived well beyond World War I, gathering fame by lyrical genius and originality, notably de la Mare, Masefield and Kipling. Notable among the War Poets to survive was Siegfried Sassoon

Realising that his eldest son was deep into poetry and often spent his evenings trying to write a poem, my father heard that Walter de la Mare was to give a series of lectures at University College, London and the great poet suggested to my father that I attended and introduced myself. I gladly queued and there followed a correspondence, which, on and off, lasted for the next twenty years. At one stage Walter de la Mare invited me to visit him at his home, Hill House in Taplow, Buckinghamshire where he gave me afternoon tea. In the course of the afternoon we discussed a phrase in one of my poems in which I mentioned that apple blossom faded and he suggested, it being late spring, that we went

5

into the garden to verify!

I am sometimes asked at what age I started actually to write verses and I suppose it was about the age of 18. These efforts had, I think, very strong echoes of de la Mare and his fellow Georgians but I remember that other things of a social nature took over in my twenties and it wasn't until close to the outbreak of World War II that I settled down seriously, circumstances permitting, to produce my juvenilia verses. For nearly ten years it seems, I had written nothing much, even experimentally. Who was it that said *'All poets die young whether they realise it nor not?'* However, when I glance at my <u>Collected</u> (1986) I see that I included nearly 40 poems which came out in my first collection, published in 1951 by the famous *Fortune Press* and which I entitled <u>Posies Once Mine</u>, immediately declaring my indebtedness to de la Mare in quoting from one of his poems. *The Fortune Press* was owned by an extraordinary man by the name of R. A. Caton who was also known to be a slum landlord in Brighton, where he had ninety-one properties, mostly without much sanitation. Philip Larkin called him a *'lazy sod'* but he did publish more than 600 books and among his authors, mainly aspiring poets, were Cecil Day-Lewis, Roy Fuller, Dylan Thomas, Philip Larkin, Kingsley Amis and Wilfred Gibson, Wallace Stevens, Thom Gunn and Martin Seymour Smith (anthologies respectively from Cambridge and Oxford). To have published so many poets with their first offerings was no mean achievement and I was absolutely delighted when in 1951 Caton brought out my first slim volume.

He engaged printers from all over the country and I see him now expostulating over a telephone on Victoria Station because printing my work was delayed. He paid no royalties and one day he arrived at my office in St James's Square with a box full of my unsold books. *'These are instead of royalties,'* he said. Timothy

D'Arch Smith in 1983* wrote a colourful and full tribute to the man he finally described as *'grim, unlovable'*. I was at least initially very unskilled in knowing how and where to submit my verses and I see that in this first collection in 1951 I could only boast of one magazine success plus two in religious periodicals.

I have on record the fact that I sold well over 100 copies of <u>Posies Once Mine</u> to family, colleagues and directors of the Life Assurance Office where I worked. My father-in-law and a local bookshop each brought a dozen copies but it was uphill work! In a sales leaflet which I produced I was allowed by Walter de la Mare to quote from a letter in which he generously said, *'I think the poems you have sent me do represent and reveal a development both in thought and in craftsmanship* and Howard Sargeant, Editor of <u>Outposts</u>, a popular poetry magazine, also allowed me to quote his comments: *'Your work has a consistent quality ... it has a discipline that is seldom seen in these days, yet you have been able to avoid the pitfalls of seeming naively.'* Professor Bonamy Dobrée was kind enough to write saying he liked the *freshness* of my verses, so I reckoned I had received sufficient encouragement to keep going.

In 1951, I had the audacity to write to John Masefield, Poet Laureate from 1930, asking him if he could influence any reviews. He kindly replied saying he liked best my poems about the East but he advised me not to be concerned about reviews adding *'in the long run, good work is found.'* In a Christmas card sent to my aunt at the Library at the time, the Laureate had included six beautiful original lines of his in <u>The Song of Caspar, the Youngest of the Three Kings</u>:

*R A Caton and the Fortune Press. Bertram Rota.

O Excellence, unthanked, unsung,
Come from Eternity to tongue
What cannot die,
Love indestructible, youth young,
Earth deep, Heaven high.

In a *Christmas Thought* for 1945, John Masefield sent to Helen –

In darkest London many years ago
A Christmas frost set-in with flakes of snow.
The lighted windows of the shops were jolly
With crackers, Christmas cards and sprigs of holly.
Lo, in the meat shop, propped upon its paws,
The pig's pale face, an orange in its jaws.
In grocer's shops the candied fruits of cost
Glistened like jewels with their toothsome frost:
Red candles lighted icing upon cake:
Some drunken waifs played "Christians, awake."

Finally, among the offerings of the laureate I found these amusing lines, preserved by my Aunt:

I have seen flowers come in stony
places
And kind things done by men with
ugly faces,
And the Gold Cup won, by the worst
horse, at the Races,
So I trust, too.

Incidentally, Henry Newbolt told my father that he thought he might well have been appointed Poet Laureate after Robert Bridges, but as the Socialist Government under Ramsey McDonald was in power the choice fell on Masefield, who had a much more rough and ready life, (notably in the Merchant Navy) than Newbolt, educated at Clifton College, Bristol

For Walter de la Mare's 80th Birthday in 1953, I sent him a poem I had written *To one who loves the Autumn*, the third verse of which went like this:

So is the passing of your days: a life
That's peaceful, childlike, bright and full of song
Draws on to dusk uncloyed, untroubled by the strife
Of gales, and may you yet your year prolong.

In thanking me for my verse, de la Mare said that although we both enjoyed that season of the year, Autumn, I had less reason to fear its significance than he had. In fact, he lived for another three years.

De la Mare had some telling things to say to me in a letter about poetry magazines and their editors, one of whom had written to me saying he *'nearly liked'* one of my poems. *'Do you suppose,'* wrote the great poet, *'that an Editor ever really realises his double responsibility; accepting contributions and refusing them!'* He added that in his own brief lifetime he had collected so many rejection slips, some in *'such fragrant terms that I could paper my bedroom with them!'* What encouragement for a minor poet!

As one tries to work the poetry magazine system, choosing the more likely journals for a particular poem, one becomes aware of editorial standards set and it would I think be fair to say that, inevitably, one editor's meat is another one's poison although it would be idle to deny that only the most original poems will find their way into A, B or C. However, magazine acceptances are certainly a good indication of the likelihood of a slim volume being accepted by a publisher, and I had to wait for a further nine years before my second slim volume appeared. Anthology appearances should definitely enhance the chances of publication and I have always been thrilled on being included in good books of that kind. Some anthologies are used as *catchpenny* efforts by minor or would-be publishers.

I am not a great believer in the value of reviews as a means of selling slim volumes. It seems that although much poetry is being written, little of it is sold. There are between 150 and 200 magazines which specialise in publishing poetry and about the same number of Poetry Presses, probably led by Bloodaxe, which publishes about thirty titles a year. When my *Collected* was published by a revived *Fortune Press* in 1986 I was awarded some pleasant reviews including one by my currently favourite magazine *Acumen*:

a minor poet who has his own distinctive lyric voice
full of the beauty of God's created world, and who has
penned a few real poems.

I think I learned my craft (or some of it anyway) by reading a large number of textbooks on the subject and I feel quite sure that I gradually took on board the dictum of T S Eliot, *'Make it new'* and therefore I commissioned myself to write verses of ungainsayable originality. One of the most testing commissions I received came in 1989 from the publisher Unwin Hyman (now part of Harper Collins) who were bringing out a new book of words and music for school assemblies, the title of which was *Wake up, stir about!* I was sent the tape of a well known tune and asked to write new words to it which I entitled *Joy to all people bring,* the final line to each verse being *'Trying hard to make the world a very much better place.'* Included in the volume were items by modem poets Wendy Cope, Patrick Dickinson, James Kirkup, U A Fanthorpe and Wes Magee, so I felt very honoured to be included. At one time in his colourful career, John Betjaman gave a reading of his work at the Royal Festival Hall and I persuaded him to read one of my favourites, his *Norfolk.* I remember the pink lining of his jacket – he was always something of a dandy, part of his charm.

In my varied experience of rejection and acceptance by editors and publishers, I recall two very satisfying but brief television appearances - the first in 1970 when the BBC exceptionally mounted a whole programme of poetry entitled *Friday Looking Sideways* and they included what they kindly described as an excellent example of descriptive verse, my *Steamer turning for Vitznau.* In 1988, ITV did a week of Epilogues of poetry and I was asked to read my own work every evening. London buses in 1994 displayed my poem on *Passive Smoking* which was also taken on by Lord McColl at Guys Hospital, as he said, in an effort to deter nurses from smoking. However, perhaps my most colourful success of earlier times was when Professor Shotaro Oshima of Waseda University in Japan put together in 1957 in the one volume, in both Japanese and English, a work entitled <u>How to Read an English Poem</u>. Many well known poets were included, Christina Rosetti, W B Yeats, Emily Dickinson, Lord Tennyson, John Keats and, of course, William Shakespeare. That one of my poems, <u>Autumn in the Nuclear Age</u> was included was, at least in part, due to memories in Japan of Hiroshima and Nagasaki, not many years earlier.

My first anthology appearance was as long ago as 1947, four years <u>before</u> my first collection and then in 1954, Michael Joseph, who published an anthology each year, included one of mine, likewise the South East Arts Association a number of times found space for one of my poems in their annual publication and *Lion* produced a volume in 1983 of <u>100 Contemporary Poets</u>, myself included. There were other minor but satisfying inclusions.

My connections with poetry would not be complete without mentioning a teaching experience I was given for about two years at Northease Manor School, Lewes, where I chaired the governing body for a number of years. The boys were all under-achievers in normal schooling and many were dyslexic but the school provided me and some boys with copies of two excellent anthologies. Although I lacked normal teaching skills, I think some of the school profited in understanding and appreciating poems. When one of the dyslexic boys achieved 'A' level in English, I took some pride but the Headmaster has since reminded me that, when I ended my teaching, I told him that I thought the experience had taught <u>me</u> more than the boys about poetry!

Turning now to my interest in hymnody, I recall with satisfaction that, in 1982, when Hodder brought out their new <u>volume</u> _Hymns for Today's Church,_ edited by Michael Baughen, then Bishop of Chester, they included my _With loving hands at work among the suffering._ It has only three verses to a tune by Professor Noel Tredinnick entitled Enigma. I attended the launch of the book in Westminster Abbey and was exceedingly pleased that my hymn, from among the 600 or so in the book, was included in the service. In 1999, this hymn was also found in _Sing Glory_, published by Kevin Mayhew together with my _We shall see him in the morning._ The collection was entitled _Hymns, Psalms and Songs for a New Century_. In the same year, Kevin Mayhew published New Start, which they described as being for '_Christian Churches of England_' in Millennium celebrations and one of my hymns was included.

I am sometimes asked a rather naive question about my poetic output: '_What things do you write about_?' The answer is equally naive –'_Anything_!'

Inevitably, there are poets who have especially captured my imagination and I suppose I would include Robert Frost, who began his poetic life in the UK before moving to the US. I was fortunate therefore to be invited several years ago, by an American Attorney, Adrian Leiby, to visit Frost's log cabin in Vermont where he wrote many poems. Included in the trip was a social occasion at Robert Frost's University, Middlebury, where he gave some of his time academically and where, once, when asked whether he thought poets were born or made, replied that _most people can't bear poets_. With very considerable hyperbole I was introduced to this gathering of academics: '_Meet Randle Manwaring. Like our Wallace Stevens, he is an insurance executive by vocation and a_ *poet by avocation.*'

I would like to make some reference to my involvement, slight though it has been, in poetry groups and I can recall with pleasure what was known as *Poets and Pints* which met at the *Lamb and Flag* in Leicester Square, London to listen to each other's poems. I am not a great believer in the value of poetry reading groups for I think it is very difficult to appreciate a new poem on hearing it read but if one can also <u>see</u> what is being read it becomes much easier to understand the poem. Some years ago, I was asked to read my work, at a meeting to the Society of Sussex Authors and I distributed, before I read, a collage of a dozen or so of my poems, which seemed to be appreciated. However, it is difficult, I believe, for poets to find a meaningful niche in literary groups – their work seems, <u>perhaps,</u> to stand apart from fiction and other writings.

I had considerable pleasure in the period 1984-1991 when Anne Lewis-Smith edited *Envoi,* a poetry journal, in being one her assistants, helping to choose the poems.

Membership of a local group, the *Downland Poets* was a mixed blessing, for rivalry and jealousy eventually elbowed me out of the chair. Nevertheless, we staged two very enjoyable readings, one of Rudyard Kipling's poems at his home in East Sussex and another the work of Hilaire Belloc at his West Sussex home.

I think it would be churlish of me unduly to criticise modern poetry but I do sincerely feel that much of it may mirror the disillusionment and depression of modern man. Personally, I find some of the poetry appearing in magazines inaccessible and even obfuscated. I fall back on a remark offered to me by a well-known literary critic who counselled me to write to be understood, implying that poets should not merely write for each other. '*Poems must say something and be about something,*' he advised from his English Chair and I believe that a minor poet has a place, even a small one, in the poetic firmament, for as William Wordsworth wrote:

If thou indeed derive thy light from Heaven,

Then, to the measure of that Heaven-born light,

Shine, Poet! in thy place and be content.

The stars pre-eminent in magnitude,

And they that from the zenith dart their beams,

(Visible though they be to half the earth,

Though half a sphere be conscious in their brightness),

Are yet of no diviner origin,

No purer essence, than the one that burns,

Like an untended watch-fire, on the ridge

Of some dark mountain; or than those which seem

Humbly to hang, like twinkling winter lamps,

Among the branches of the leafless trees.

Table of Contents

A Time of War

A Time for Sport

A Time of Unbelief

The Still Sad Music

Time's Wingèd Chariot

Chestnuts

Now that your glorious youth has passed away
And the dark splendour of the foliage green
Has fallen down through each succeeding day,
What shall remind us of your beauty seen
With joy, by us, when all the earth was young,
When her long anthem was but half unsung?

There was a time, when there beneath your shade
We rested, lulled in nature's wonderland
When your rough leaves above, a music made
And shadows danced before us, idly planned.
Then bees would pass us by in zigzag flight,
Filling the air with murmurings of delight.

Though once your leaves, so thickly set, forbade
Our eyes to gaze up at the heavenly scene,
Autumn has left you bare and slowly made
Small windows where the darkened roof has been,
And only brown and gold now decorate,
Your lovely house where summer dwelt of late.

Now nothing but the raindrops' gentle sound
Falling and trembling from leaf to twig, will mourn
The days gone by. And yet upon the ground,
Between the leaves and grasses, there is born
A wondrous thing – a chestnut brown and white,
Shining and new, and stored with summer's light.

The Hill

Upwards goes the burning track
    tireless feet have taken,
Up to where, beneath the moon
    Heaven's boughs are shaken:
Where the dews come, dropping down
    Slowly through the branches,
Bending the slender russet leaves,
    Dewy avalanches.

There the dreamer dreams no more,
    There are dreams forgotten:
All he hoped for longingly,
    of his sleep begotten,
There is beauty on the hill
    Slumbers, fading never,
And his crown of thorn is there
    Cast away for ever.

When Evening Comes

Evening now: come out and see
The shadows creep on Beacon Hill.
When black-wing night is drawing near,
A star comes through beside the mill.

And there below the starlit ridge,
Against the dimness of the sky
And brooding on earth's peacefulness,
Silhouetted cattle lie.

So evening comes across the fields
And calls the bat and beetle out,
Until the owl on silent wings
Has scattered all with maddened shout.

Boyhood

O soul that roams the Southern Hills,
O peace among the flowers,
O joy that with the lightest step
Goes romping through the showers!

O friend in windy days of March
When fields are green with rain,
O heart that fears the joyful spring
Will not return again!

All you were mine for one long hour
In Boyhood long ago;
But now, I fear with each new day
You less familiar grow.

Summer Nightfall

The last low beams of sunlight fall
    Across the sea,
And far away the sunset pales;
    Night comes to me

The silvered sands grow dimmer; every rock
Is silent where the waves with sounding shock
    Forerun the tide;
The shore is now deserted, east and west
And every strange sea-bird has flown to rest,
    The Channel wide.

Now not one lingering boy strays there beside
The sea, to watch the gentle tossing tide
    The seaweed drown;
And not a ship or sail moves into sight;
All lies most peaceful; in the failing light
    The sun goes down.

Voices

I know a sanctuary, away
From all the sounds of restless day,
Where silence reigns awhile, till comes
The music of a thousand drums,
Which stirs the silent voices there
As softest singing fills the air;
Then as the drums' grand music dies
Shrill tunes from joyful pipes arise
And join with welling songs of joy
The overflowing hearts employ,
Their youthful spirit to impart
To him who comes with burdened heart.

And when asleep, I hear the sound
Of voices hushed and memory-bound;
And far away, the slightest breeze,
For me brings singing to the trees.

Other Eyes

Grow old, dear hills, and no more waste
Your lovely green on other eyes;
Grow old in autumn, in your haste
Forget the spring and that there lies
   Another year ahead of this.
Grow old, my vales and fields of green,
Then fade from sight all summer flowers,
For there are eyes which have not seen
Your beauty in the evening hours;
   The beauty they for ever miss.

Then die, bright birds, songsters die
Who sang for us through countless years;
But now I would your song should fly
And fall no more on other ears;
   For there your song remains unheard.
Fall down, loved stars, and leave the night
To all her darkness evermore,
And hide both sun and moon your light,
Fall not again on sea or shore
   Or on the breast of any bird.

And clouds that grace the summer blue
With rainbows of new-born earth,
There were many times when you
Quite failed to give the wonder birth
   In hearts that knew you passed along.
So vanish clouds, all beauty go
And leave awhile a darkened world;
Then suddenly, where none shall know
Come back, and ever, leave unfurled
   Man's wonder in your sudden song.

Farewell

I say farewell to those dear hills
  And fields where swiftest martins play;
I say farewell to darkened mills
  On shining banks when fades the day.
Farewell, I bid, because no more
  Shall we with you old pathways take
Nor roam the long deserted shore,
  Where waves yet break.

The rocks and smooth untrodden sand,
  Long afternoons we walked in peace;
Though this was once to you a land
  Of magic, where we found increase
Of pleasure in discovery;
  To rocks in tears I say farewell
But know that in the heart of me
  They leave their spell.

It is for you, this sad good-bye,
  Who nevermore at night shall see
The moon across the downs go high
  Nor stars that linger furtively;
Who shall not walk with us again
  To villages in valleys fair
Nor smell the soft-sweet summer rain
  And scented air.

For you who live beyond the west
      I say farewell to those things bright
That live where once you took your rest;
      Where once you bathed in summer light;
They do not fade, our Sussex flowers
      Which not again your hands shall touch;
They live for us who through long hours
      Shall count them much,

The orchards where the apples swing
      Beside the cornfields of the vale,
Shall blossom with returning spring
      And we shall watch their colour pale.
Such time is past for you who call
      No more by name the Traveller's Joy
Which hung on nature's orchard well,
      In her employ.

And you that left the hills of home
      To seek the cities of the plain
Will you not remember as you roam
      Not us, but Beauty born in vain.
The mornings when the fields rejoice,
      The green, the flowers and every bird,
All these to you had once a voice,
      But now unheard!

The Unremembered

When in the silent dark I lie,
In thought to linger with the light,
Days moments, slowing circling, fly
And pass again before my sight.

Then scenes returning to the mind
Alive with colour, strength and grace,
I see but dreamily outlined,
And each remembered friendly face.

But there are features lost in dream
And by no conscious effort wrought
Which, though beloved, forever seem
Transfixed beyond my furthest thought.

The Enchanted Lake – Wandsworth Common

One day the rustic bridge came down
And they built a safer one of stone,
With disenchantment in a world
Where childhood kept the feast alone.

We fished the edge or weedy depths,
Bright stickleback or minnow found-
In summers when the lake was dry
We trod upon forbidden ground.

We watched the rhododendrons blaze
And swans desert their lofty nest,
With coots and moorhens hurrying
By leaves and osiered banks caressed.

A half-sunk punt moored by the bridge,
Grown old in slime and gossamer,
Once crossed to the island sanctuary
When Ulysses sailed to Ithaca.

After the Visit
(Hardyesque)

Unconsciously seeking
but never finding –
    a waiting game,
    played blindfold –
hoping against no hope,
he found, from time to time,
unexpected treasure.

Nostalgia

She was always speaking of those days:
clothes rationing, utility furniture
and a pint of milk for a penny halfpenny.

No washing machines, fridges or freezers –
literally living from hand to mouth;
no *'best buy'*, *'sell by'*, pesticides, check-outs.

Blitz and bombing and home-grown food,
making do for weddings and baby things –
what a struggle it was in the hard old days.

He grew rather tired of the prices she quoted
and once hit back – *'that was a day*
when you could be run over by a horse and cart.'

Smoking

From rising bell to slow lights out
suffocating fumes crawl round
fleshy dungeons of the lungs
      taking in each other's smoke.

In every room residual whiffs
swirl and cling, settling down
in curtains, chairs, everywhere
      taking in each other's smoke.

Marking the future fight for breath,
ash falls in grey fragility
making no choice between man and wife
      taking in each other's smoke.

Ageing

Who drew the tell-tale lines and when
      engraved each fatal story,
     then silently at a secret hour
     robbed of a lifetime's glory?
Impish hands, never caught in the act,
      settled death's irreversible fact.

In The Psychiatric Ward

Thin walls divide
the living from the living –
no tell-tale uniform
of brisk officiousness.

Thin walls divide
the loving from the loved;
a quiet mind
in one but not the other.

Thin walls divide
psychosomatic
from the normal
heart-breaks of life.

Thin walls divide
the psychopath
from the psychiatrist's
near normality.

Poliomyelitis

Down sixty years of strain I follow him
    And see his steel-girt flesh is never freed,
Who drags about a feeble, fettered limb
    With sinews shrunk and muscles atrophied.

He may not run or fall as other boys,
    Nor manly thrill of swerve and dash may feel;
He will not know the ease of earthly joys
    Yet, in his soul, the deepest wounds may heal.

To One Who Loves the Autumn
(For Walter de la Mare, 1953)

The gentlest autumn in tempestuous years
Has come and touches flowers and fruit and leaves;
This fall has come without her cries and tears
And silently her coloured curtain weaves.

How softly drop the last of summer's joys,
No gales strip branches naked in a night,
No frost the curled chrysanthemum destroys;
The sun prolongs our open-air delight.

So is the passing or your days; a life
That's peaceful, childlike, bright and full of song
Draws onto dusk uncloyed, untroubled by the strife
Of gales, and may you yet your year prolong.

Last Night of the Proms, 1967
(remembering Sir Malcolm Sargent)

We were so glad you came to pay
your tribute to the music you
adorned these many years.

The splendid season, with its Bach and Brahms,
Elgar and Holst, Sibelius and the rest,
has come and gone; attention has been rapt
for soloist and orchestra alike.
The boys and girls in promenading styles
with older people in their stalls and boxes
joined to acclaim, in music's festival,
the triumph of the spirit over fear,
the world uniting mysteries of tune
and all the noble victories of song.
Wood-wind and brass, strings and percussion
met in a welcome of the man they knew,
who in these two decades had made his life
a favourite concerto.

We were so glad you came, surprising us,
to make up something of the lack we felt,
missing so long the magic of your touch.

Pine Forest

Among the towering pines
of perennial pride,
falling but not fallen,
the mossy path astride,
adding a new dimension,
one leans across the ride.

Caught at sixty degrees,
it makes a special mark
with shafts of angled light
in the criss-cross dark,
dead amongst the living
lying bark to bark.

When will it fall completely,
all support withdrawn
by neighbour pines,
their roots outworn,
on a brushwood couch
to be stripped and sawn?

We stand together now
silent among the trees,
wondering at the limit
of life's harmonies,
as the wind, passing over,
another death decrees.

Immanence

When spring walks silently
across the heath, along the hills,
I feel again
in flowers and children's laughter
the immanence of love, the urgency
and thrust of life.

From celandine
and lark-song spiralling
the healing waters flow
to bring a Lazarus
to life. The word, the touch
build strength and poise
symmetrically.

Old Counties

Farewell
To the lakes and mountains,
The rugged places
Of Westmorland;
To quiet towns,
Oakham and Uppingham,
In smallest Rutland.

Now
We must search
In Cumbria
And Leicestershire
For those dear names
From vanished counties
Swept into history.

Steamer Turning for Vitznau
at Weggis, Switzerland

(This is the most charming place I have ever lived in.
Mark Twain)

There is a moment of perfection
when a beautiful woman turns
and moves away; seconds later
you recall the magic instant
of fast receding glory.
>   And there is a day of graduation
>   when years of learning fall away;
>   he turns and walks, applauded, smiling
>   to ultimate success or failure; parents
>   remember their day of exultation.

There is the moment of setting course
when, shrugging off the landing stage,
the steamer turns away from the shore,
from the carpet of mauve taulonia blossom,
turns from the music of Strauss and Lehar.
>   She reaches out for the shelter of Rigi,
>   for the trees and mountains above Weggis
>   and this a moment of lakeside perfection
>   the morning sun dancing in proud attendance
>   as the steamer turns for the arms of Vitznau.

The Fiddler of Weggis

He makes Weggis unique
among lakeside resorts
for there, through every season,
he plays with poise and gusto,
   throwing himself, with violin
   into all melodies
   of the western world
   from Strauss to Lloyd Webber.
Urbane in the extreme,
he will dance in ecstasy
melting distant snows
above the summer snow-line.

As leader of the trio
he provides a marked charisma,
a Maurice Chevalier
panache for each performance,
   while unattached, middle-aged
   women provide warm
   and constant adulation,
   as he smiles his winning way
through every lakeside concert,
singing the German songs
sotto voce, double-bass, piano
in obedient obligato.

Parade of the Steamers, Luzern

Sailing like old swans, they take the centre
stage, in proud remembrance of the days
 when singly, they crissed-crossed the lake.

Now, on the launching date of a re-made ship,
they come again, full team, in line abreast,
 decked overall, to celebrate.

Another season starts as a pale May sun
dapples the calm where an armada of ships
 follows the festive fleet of five.

Helicopters buzz the whole convoy,
chatter with hungry gulls at funnel height
 answering the hooting of the veterans.

A holiday crowd along the promenade,
where chestnut candelabra mark the spring,
 joins in celebration.

Ageless snows on regal Mount Pilatus
welcome the paddle steamers' whirring wings,
 whispering Edwardian elegance.

Uri, Pride of the Fleet – Lake Lucerne, 2004

In her one hundred and two years,
    steaming her way to greatness,
    flying her country's flag
with chimney in proud, slanting style,
paddles obedient to clanking crankshafts,
    which shine in timeless power,
    She survives every invention,
a model of a country's perfection.

King's College Chapel, Cambridge

More than a cathedral in many ways,
for five hundred years a masterpiece,
always but annually, in particular,
music reverberating round the world
with words both ancient and modern,
composers living and dead echoing
the Royal but humble Nativity.

Perpendicular and gothic in style,
timeless in truth and symbolism,
choir and congregation blend
though the lessons, readings and carols
with dean, a fellow, a student and staff
joining in single proclamation –
this the uniqueness of the Chapel.

Coned Off

Stay in the outside lane
as long as you can
till headlights flash
from the harrying man.

Coned off, move over
to the middle way,
in middle age
for a while to stay.

But the cones will get you
once again
in single file
to the inside lane.

The motorway ends
in one mile, to become
tediously suburban
all the way home.

Magpies

One's sorrow, two's mirth,
Three's a wedding, four's a birth,
Five's a christening, six a dearth –
     So the old rhyme tells.
Whatever are the auguries
Of our ancient mysteries,
Shakespeare called them magotpies
     And feared their magic spells.

The Village Wedding

I

By Chipping Hill the wide fields lie
Bounded by ditch, low hedge and wire
Through scattered farmlands where the spring
Sweeps onward into Cambridgeshire.

The skylark rises to the light
In loneliness and greyness where
The young corn springing in the blade
Lends colour to the waiting year.

Amongst the sheltering elms the rooks
Have built high nests above the farm
Resting in silence in the noon,
Knowing no hurry or alarm.

The old sow feeds contentedly
Beyond the blossom and daffodil;
A labourer moves across the yard
Unstirred his heart in this April.

II

Upstairs the bridal party dress
And laugh and chatter with the bride.
She is ready for whom the day was made;
The white veiled radiance of her face
Is now the glory of the house.

Outside, in the lanes, the trudge of a man's feet
And the patter of a woman's going home
Alone disturb the noontide quiet
But about the church the people gather
Where uncertain sunshine occasionally
Lights up the guests and the limousines
In which they have travelled from distant shires;
Sir William and Lady Montefiore,
Aunt Catherine and Uncle Max,
The nurse from a London hospital
As well as the couples from Surrey and Kent
Who really know the bridal pair.

On the green before the church
The geese feed on obliviously:
From distant cottages the villagers,
Blue suited, cloth capped, have come to see
The wedding. They came to the sound of the bells,
The golden bells of Edgar Allan Poe,
To Baldock and to Royston calling
Insistently, that all may know.

III

Five bells call from the embattled tower
      Proclaiming the everlasting day
Of a later Gothic edifice
      Buttressed against death and decay;

Six centuries of burn and blot
      Have left her ancient ministry
Unsullied in the age-long fight
      For Christian faith and piety.

Now tower and chancel, and aisle
      Are vibrant with the noise of bells;
The sound which Housman hated once
      A gladder story now foretells.

The organist plays softly through
      The tumult of the chiming praise,
Ten choir boys dress, prepare to sing
      The psalms and hymns of wedding days.

IV

'Praise, my soul, the King of heaven'
Bursts forth as the procession moves
Slowly from porch to the chancel steps
She has come to the church whom every eye
Has waited long to see. She comes,
Serene in her bridal gown
With perfect poise, majestically.
The shepherd of the country flock
Smiles down upon the bride and groom
Who face him almost nervously,
Expectantly. The music stops.
He speaks the words of Christian power:
'Of the holy estate of matrimony
Into which these two now come to be joined'
He speaks of the mutual comfort they will find
And the blessings of children, their nurture
In the admonition of the Lord.

V

The pale light of an April day
Seems changed to dazzling brilliance
As man and maid are here pronounced
One; transfigured in the blaze of union,
Hallowed within the marriage vows
They stand hands linked, hearts joined,
Each conscious most in this moment's peace
Of the other in the shining morning of love.

'The Lord's my Shepherd, I'll not want'
We sing, and pray for those united here.

VI

The register is signed beyond
The choir stalls in the chancel,
The laughter and talk of the families
Mingle with the organ's music
Before the procession moves down
The nave, while the congregation
Eye furtively the two made one,
Swept forward in the Wedding March.
While cameras click and lace and veil
Flutter in the breeze, the guests glide out
And cross the churchyard mounds which hide
The honoured dead of centuries
And slowly move through villagers,
Gathered about the old lychgate.

VII

Thus to the Hall, across a countryside
Empty in this later afternoon.
There lawns are trimmed and borders gay
With tulips and forget-me-nots
Wallflowers and narcissus.
The guests pass through the house, greeting
And being greeted by parents and the two,
Then out into the garden where a large marquee
Is spread surely in the uncertain weather.
There the merry crowd jostle and talk
And drink to the health of the bride and groom,
She beautiful and calm, he triumphant,
Together they cut the cake, while the laughter blurs
Into animation which sways us all.

VIII

The father will know her no more
As the daughter of his house;
She is going forever to be his
Who has won her and made her his own.
They will sit, the old people, beside the fire
And dream of the girl she was
In pigtails and picture hat;
She will come back to them, back to the farm
On another day when summer has spread
Garlands before her homing feet,
But now the dusk comes over the land she knew,
Closing the day of her maidenhood,
As she goes, exultant on love's full tide.

At a London Terminus

A photograph fell, as a sycamore seed
Or an autumn leaf but none gave heed
To that stranger's face and the jostling throng
At the platform barrier rushed along,
Fighting its way to the seats on the train.
Trampled and blackened by the mire and the rain,
The portrait's features expressionless grew
Beneath the heels and hidden from view
By a heedless world like a battle-scarred
Soldier in death, his outline marred.
And who was she, some girl who let slip
One late afternoon, fixed eye, mute lip
And shining face? Did she cherish in pain
His memory, he who had died, not in vain?
Did she think of him with many more
Or write each week to a foreign shore?
Maybe she grieved now he was wed
And another maid to the altar had led.
Perchance to the flames, she would often debate,
To consign this scrap and obliterate
All that she knew of a day gone by
And now it was done remorselessly,
So perhaps it was best she should brood no more,
This wound might heal as it could not before...
The signals winked to the trains on their way,
The photograph gone and the girl in grey.

Dilemma

There was a man who said that he
    Was undenominational;
He smote the sects of this and that,
    (Deploring the sensational);

He hated ritual and the ruts
    Of churches in the High Street,
So joined himself with others such
    In quarters down a by-street

Their clandestine foregatherings
    Were mentioned quite *sub-rosa*,
But people passing by would think:
    'They've set themselves a poser,

For all their efforts to set up
    A non-sectarian basis,
May force, well, even them, at last
    To *name* their new oasis'.

The Bitter and Frustrating Years

How much they loved, how long they loved,
    A stranger cannot tell
Nor what despairing midnights known
    Under the ancient spell
But now it seems a little thing,
    The loving touch or word,
Since time has ravaged both their hearts
    And no more songs are heard.

Life as the ever roaring stream
    Bears all our loves away,
Leaving the many kindnesses
    Stark in the autumn day;
Only a few are crying still
    Down by the edge of the wood,
Kissing the stones to life again
    As the river turns to blood.

Tout Passe

I met a lady of Charlton Kings
who graved *tout passe* on one of her rings.

Her husband was a sailing man
who put to sea in a catamaran.

Sometimes he found his love afloat,
crewed for the summer in a larger boat.

The wife came to St Mawes in July,
watched his sailing with a critical eye;

saw him in lantern-lit cafés,
confirming the parting of their ways.

Her eavesdropping ended, she read her rings
and took her own life in Charlton Kings.

Imperatives

Love is all,
        friendship nearly;
missing both
        we suffer dearly.

Unfinished Business
(Marriage)

There are some who should be
and many who would be,
some who should not be
yet, those who are, entered
with highest hopes.

Honeymoons are always brief
some unexpectedly very
and even those who co-habit
find the eventual not
quite what they hoped for.

On our faces we write the story,
elation, contentment, pain;
unreturning, unremitting
years become explicit
and cannot be undone.

It is nature's festival,
a shower of stars, the fact
of two becoming one,
the romances of youth
outshining other loves.

In the tear-stained troughs,
or sun-drenched uplands,
in heart, mind and will
souls blend in unconscious
making and mending.

All earthbound pleasures are found
somewhere in the marriage bond,
friendship high on the agenda,
bodies expressively giving
their answers in the yes and no.

But whatever the exhilaration
of love in earthy form,
strawberries and cream
will be surpassed
in an unbelievable other life.

No longer a need to preserve
the human race, they neither
marry nor are given in marriage,
the communication of all souls,
as angels, incorruptible.

A Time of War

Betrothal, 1941

On this glad day of love declared and won
I'll make a sonnet and a song for you
To tell of all the thoughts which, old and new
Pass by; of days when love had but begun
To change the dying summer into spring,
To burn its beacon through the blackened night,
Until each moment with unfading light
Was slowly filled, love's permanence to bring.

I'll tell you that no storm or cloud shall change
The beauty of the path which we shall tread;
Though war might hover long years overhead
It cannot one moment us estrange;
Love shall live bravely, brightly. With a kiss
We vow and find therein undying bliss.

Embarkation Leave, 1944

Back from the strong and tireless arms
Of wife and children, now must go
The soldier sworn to victory:
He feels awhile their love and warms
His heart, which soon must overflow
With tears that none could ever see.

In these bright, scurrying days he felt
A peace unsullied by the strife –
Forgotten are those marching feet –
And here the unfettered spirit dwelt
To learn again the art of life,
In war's surcease, a bitter sweet.

Now to the fight where nations fall
Headlong across the eastern sea,
The warrior goes without a name;
Hears into the distance many a call
Sent from a global threnody
And answering sails, with the world aflame.

Convoy, 1944

Suddenly we felt the kind soft air
Blowing across the sea
And there was laughter everywhere;
Spent then the storm and turned to fair
Was the changeling world to me.

Over the waves where the dark must shroud
Great Ships in the tropic night
The moon from her space beneath a cloud
Flecks silver the waves and spume is endowed
With phosphorescent light.

After much easting with Africa nigh
Offshore all captains must wait;
While feluccas unfurl against the sky,
Brown skins, red capped, are passers-by
And all pass through the orient gate.

Premonition in Burma

We heard you sing the songs of France
    In the mess at midnight,
While the parched earth bathed her burning face
    Under the starlight.

The tent was filled with memories
    As your fingers strayed
Over the strings of the guitar,
    So easily you played.

Next day we stood beside your grave
    Carved in the mountain side,
Remembering the liberty
    For which you died.

The trumpet sounded and the fire
    Of rifles smote the air.
(How fearlessly a man last night
    Of death became aware).

Thoughts from Rangoon
August 1945

I was away last spring
On the torrid plains
Of Mandalay:
I saw the city burn and fall
Under the stars
And watched the slow unhurried trail
Of creaking cars
Beyond Shwebo,
Patiently, in the cruel heat
Returning home.
Still there was colour, strength and song
In the Burmese heart
And a concert given
By their loyal troops and dancing girls
In the cool of night
On the arid waste
At Ondaw. The strip was quiet
And free from ops.
That was in March;
No blossom and no English green
Was there; no Devon lane
All primroses or wood
Thick with violets soft and dark
On Surrey hills.
Now people talk
Of going East to Bangkok and Saigon –
Chinese Cafés
and less rain.
But give me back before next Spring
My English soil,
When new life's afoot
At Massingham and Marlborough,
After the wind
Gentle and warm,
Clears the snow from the roads at home.

Kalimpong

We flew
Over the jungle and into Bengal,
Landing, across the muddy river
And the flat, white roofs outside Calcutta;
Thence in a train, northwards and upwards,
Leaving the burning plains behind –
Skywards and onwards in the small, slow train,
Climbing the foothills of the Himalayas;
And further by road to Kalimpong,
On the Eastern borders of shuttered Nepal.
There, tired by the heat and the long monsoon,
We listened again to the music of poetry,
Drank of the far glories of Kanchinjinga
At dawn, as she lay in eternal snows
And there we felt in our hearts a revival.
The delicious coolness of evening air
Came back with its benison to make us forget
The sweat of the sweltering nights in Rangoon.

A Memory of VJ Day, Rangoon

Law Po Chye, the restaurateur,
Stood in the Court House until noon;
Under his walnut skin there burned
A spirit dimmed by the long monsoon.

Corporal Snooks and Corporal Snod,
Charged with menacing old Po Chye,
Bursting with indignation stand,
While the time of the white man passes by.

Whither

When the flickering present lies grey in ashes
And her gipsying years are a county away,
Will they remember this straggling encampment's
Discordant sounds at the close of a day?

They will have built, in the fields, to-morrow,
Towns for their trading and a road to the sea
Where the Romany children sing together
Or burn to death by a blistered tree.

Autumn In The Nuclear Age

Swiftly the summer passes
    On swallow's wings,
Murmuring the mass migration
    Of living things.

Slowly the curtain closes
    On earth's festival
Promising other roses
    While petals fall.

Soon, in the splendid evening,
    As the last hope dies,
A new, undreamed creation
    Through flames will rise.

A Time for Sport

Cricket Season

April and the beeches in tiny leaf;
the grass, lush green and recovering
from recent rains. The amphitheatre
in perfect trim; flags of West Indies
and the Duke saluting the weakling sun.
Along the valley the Arun snakes
and in the dim grey distances
the downs, surrounding all.

A family day; children in the woods;
small girls wear daisy chains for coronets;
everyone queues for ices or beer;
(music by the band of the Grenadier Guards).

Shouting advice: 'Watch it, Seymour',
West Indians gesticulate
with outstretched pink palms or waving score cards,
as if they made a fighting speech.

On the Saffrons ground the summer slips
slowly away in the holiday crowd;
the dark blue Sussex flag against
the darkening leaves of August end.

Like a ball a swallow skims the turf;
a dragon-fly zig-zags in the sun,
while the bell of the Eastbourne Civic Hall
sounds the death-knell of another season

The Club Man

Every club needs one but only one.
He is the answer to every whim;
helps at the bar, stacks the chairs,
shouts to a player, 'Steady, Jack!'
and calls his fellow members 'lads.'

He moves around at quite a pace
and even in the hottest weather
sports the club tie; the embodiment
of social life, chain-smoking and
beer-bellied, clubbable, alone.

Cricket Final

Gloucestershire and Somerset,
finalists at Lords,
join in friendly joust,
        knocking down the stumpy.

From Cotswolds and Blackdown Hills,
from Quantocks and the Mendips,
from Forest of Dean and Bristol,
        they came with ale and scrumpy.

Botham, Garner and Richards,
plus Grace, Graveney and Procter,
watching, made each others' rides
        very distinctly bumpy.

Limited Overs

Cricketers know that limited over
matches end eventually.
So with matches between the male
and female; they may go on full term
or end in had light, rough weather or death.
They are the perfect but temporary answer.

The squads on which they are based grow;
the overs build up – all overs soon over –
bowled with guile or ferocity,
producing the climate of the game,
while totals flickering on the board
record the skills of both sides in the match.

Locked in the middle for the whole
of the contest, the over rate quickens;
applause is given for entertainment;
there is no championship as such
but in the best matches each side
will award the other bonus points.

Children of the Regiment

A few years ago, as girls, they watched
furtively, half-interested, reading a book
then, with marriage to a county hero,
each settled for being a cricketing wife.

Now, with their babies, they continue watching
at home matches, engrossed in the welfare
of the little ones but when their men come home
from away fixtures just deal with dirty washing.

Once, their grandmothers, sent back to England
for their education, were children of another regiment,
the males serving at Simla or Snooty Ooty
and playing polo for the Bengal Lancers.

Wives of the county team, they enjoy a fame
for a few swift summers while husbands keep
a place in the premier side, with children
of once competing women and competitive males.

The Holiday Month

This is the season of the year
When, in the northern hemisphere,
The people leaving their work behind,
New health and relaxation find
In an established health resort
Or following a hobby or sport
Or flying off to the south of France
Or camping near Aix-en-Provence,
Visit Spain or the Berlin wall
Or crewed for a race to Portugal.

But the family man goes down to the sea,
Sand-castling, canoeing, sun-bathing goes he
For fourteen days at the holiday game
He exercises his bronzing frame.

The Flower Show

Choosing this year's Beauty Queen is such a task,
For the hotel staff (filling-in for a year) are shy
And it leaves only three or four from which to choose,
The plain and the Jane, the Jill and the daffodil.

Pray silence for her to open the Flower Show
But where is the Chairman of the organizing Committee?
We need him to introduce the Beauty Queen.
He is red-faced, grey-suited, pink buttonholed:
He staggers across to the microphone:
She giggles and smiles and is cheered on her way
With her attendants who rank close second and third.

These are the flowers of the August Festival:
Gladioli, asters, roses and late delphinium,

French marigold, sweet peas, and red-hot pokers;
Marrows and beans, tomatoes and lettuce.
Prize labels are planted by the judges already;
Children jostle the crowd and hurry round
In the cool of the marquee, the cool of the shade,
Where the cacti, embroidery, knitting and cakes
Are laid out in sections, class one, two or three.

Now step outside to the bowling alley
And bowl the balls for a sucking pig.
Throw the quoits at those sensational prizes,
Guess the weight of a large Dundee cake;
The Charming attendant will take your name.
Come, shove the ha'penny and knock down a coconut;
Six shies for threepence and ladies half-way;
The fun of the fair in the seaside air.

We must remember that this is the flower show;
The marquee invites to its quiet, shady peace
Away from the skittles, the shouts, the loud-speaker,
We are back with the cucumbers, the cress and the jam.

The Cricket Match

The captain, retired Commander, R.N.,
Raises his team of local worthies.
There is Barlow the barman to open the innings
Plus Smithers, who once played for the Army
And for the Stragglers of Asia in Hong Kong;
Three men from the farms, cross batted and strong,
Fast bowlers, fast scorers, good fielders, all,
Good losers, fierce enemies year by year.
There is Murdoch, the only taxi-driver,
A pretty good wicket-keeper with spin;
Young Anderson, in the first at Stowe,

Jenkins and Maxwell from the village stores.
It's always a problem to find the eleventh
But the visitors, our opponents always supply
A middle-aged man they hardly need.

Now the hotel side is usually strong,
On paper at least, but the pitch gets most
Club players out for a very few runs;
The young men complain at length of the plantains
And the lack of a sight-screen across the pinetrees.
But in the dark-blue shirts and khaki shorts
They fling their bats at the bowling in style –
Throw away the batting gloves at thirty
And cast away your wicket after that.

For Commander Henfrey Hallett must not lose,
He is Chairman of the urban District Council,
And life-long member of the M.C.C:
From his mid-off vantage point he crouches
As the sun goes down across the bay.
He pounces on the umpires with a shout
When victory, sweet victory comes into view:
He has not lost since fifty-six.

The Regatta

The sixteenth annual regatta
Is held in the Small Bay for most of the day
(By kind permission of the lord of the manor)
And in command for the whole proceedings
Is Captain Aubrey Featherstone Haugh,
Shouting across the peaceful water,
His iron commands to sailors and swimmers.
Will that launch with the lady in blue slacks
Please move out of the way. Thank you.'

The proceeds of the regatta will be given
To Village Social organizations,
So enter now for the competitions
And step up now to the platform where the judges
Will give their verdict on the Bathing Beauties;
Miss Veronica Plantrose, the well known film star,
In faded, brittle celluloid beauty,
Will present the valuable prizes in person.
O Veronica, in the autumn of her discontent,
Attended by Fi-fi, her little pet poodle,
Attended also by some ancient glamour boys
Who fawn on her splendidly aging form.

And if you spot the litter lout
You may win a pound by challenging him.
The in-shore events, the rowing, the swimming
Are in full-swing in the dazzling sun;
For the adults – a water derby race
And a novelty fancy-dress parade.
King Neptune and his merry wives arrive
From across the bay in seaweed drapery
With cocoa-plastered, gleaming faces
And the children haul their boat ashore.

As the afternoon drags on, the sailing
For the Gorringe Cup and the King Flower Vase;
Enterprise and Firefly, Dayboat and Albacore,
Sail into the dim blue distances,
Sail on their long triangular course,
While the crowds dwindle along the shore;
They are looking forward to 'the dance of the year',
Held in the Village Memorial Hall,
Dancing to the music of Paddy Burns
And his ever-popular orchestra.
So leave the ships sailing and the committee struggling
To bring the regatta to a proper conclusion.

The highlights and sideshows of August are over
And the families go from the Pine Wood Hotel,
From the dinghies, the beach huts, the water-skiing,
Back to the sameness, the circle at home
And the long winter evenings of colour slides.

Lords

Oxford blue caps of England under a Cambridge sky
        Here in high summer, ladies in straws or coolies;
Men in old caps, homburgs, trilbies or bowlers,
        Open necks, Etonian and I.Z. ties.

This is a land at peace between her wars –
        These the survivors of Tobruk and Gallipoli;
The colonels, the clerks, the farmers and the engineers,
        Who pay with their pounds and their blood for
                the home of the free.

Here mingle club captains, their umpires and those on
        Committees,
        The hard-hitting parson away from his village
        cricket;
The members, the maidens, the boys, the bores and
        the blues
        To see England at play, attacking, defending –
                a wicket.

A Time of Unbelief

The Way He Came

To a country which passed like a penny piece
from Assyria to Rome via Persia and Greece
in seven hundred years, new meaning He gave
when thirty silver coins bought a Roman slave.

In a rough, rustic home He grew up with the others,
with their plans and their pains and the sins of His
        brothers;
in the carpenter's shop through sadness and joy,
He lighted the tasks with the zest of a boy.

In a quiet hill-town he came to manhood,
barley loaves and fish their staple food
with a few figs and honeycomb the occasional luxury;
through this simplicity, He entered humanity.

Centuries of worldly pomp and prejudice,
fighting and fear, hatred and caprice
have taken us far from His incarnation,
the down-to-earth coming of God, in his Son.

His Hands

With loving hands,
At work among the suffering
And broken hearts, He ministers,
Who is their King.

With wounded hands,
Outstretched upon a Jewish tree,
He lies and then is lifted up
In agony.

With pleading hands,
Towards the world He longs to bless,
He waits, with heaven's life to fill
Man's emptiness.

Yokes

"I made that yoke", said Jesus, as
He walked. "I and my earthly father
also made the plough you see."

When, later, as a man He strode
across those fields, He offered all
the yoke if His discipleship.

But after three and thirty years,
His manly shoulders bore, alone,
upraised, a single Roman yoke.

It was the one He willingly
took to Himself when carrying,
to death, the sin of all the world.

The War of The Cross

He fought alone for us, as God,
The fiercest battle that the world
Has ever seen. Not Marathon
Or Hastings or Orleans saw
Such vital victory as when
He slew man's enemy
And wrested from him power
To hold and kill and keep.
No Waterloo or Blenheim field
Witnessed such clash of arms
Decisively as this,
The climax of the wars, where right
Throws off the yoke of ill,
And no Armada's fleet
Came forward with such might
As this, when powers of hell
And principalities
Holding dominion in the air,
The rulers of the darkness
Of this night, hurled onward.
The hierarchy of Evil,
Once had secured
Such spoils, mankind and creation.

Plundered from God and pillaged from man,
Held always in their grip
Now were intent on retaining
Their mastery in the world,
While the air was thick with doom and death
On the green hillside.

The task before the Son of God
Was greater than all the deeds
Of Hercules or Samson;

Crueller far than ancient chains
Was that of death and sin
Which on the cross he broke;
Nobler, His deeds than conquerors,
Than Alexander who
Threw off the Persian yoke
Through all the lands
As far as the River Indus.

Man's ancient foe came on,
Some Hector, to be slain at length
By Him, greater in strength than Achilles
Who dragged dark Hector's body round,
Thrice round the walls of Troy.
But He, the Lord, through bloody sweat,
Wishing the hour might pass from Him
And that bitter cup of human guilt
Might somehow be removed,
Strove in the hour of darkness.

There, at the end of the Roman world,
Outstretched between the earth and sky
He hung, dying a villain's death,
Crushed by the weight of grief
And human sin. At the heart of the old
Decaying religion and life
He died, surrounded by priests and soldiers
Condemned by the culture of Greece,
The might of Rome and the Jews.
The prince of darkness was there,
Arrayed in his vestures of purple
But the Warrior of Heaven fought
Despoiling the governments
And the vile authorities
Arraigned against His rule.

As a wrestler cast from him
His beaten antagonist
In the games of ancient Greece
So He, strong Son of God
Defeating in His death
The strong one armed, threw from Him
His defeated foe, making a show
Openly on His bitter Cross;
The convict's gibbet thus became
The Victor's glorious chariot.

The wickedness which fixed
His body to a Jewish tree,
He smote as in divine revenge,
Turning upon His enemy
And nailing it to the cross;
Thus He in mortal combat slew
The enemies of the souls of men,
Death, wickedness and hell.

Like a Roman general,
Returning from the wars
And carrying in his train
The trophies of his victory,
Pausing from place to place
To celebrate be-garlanded,
The triumphs of the battlefield,
He came, back from the Cross,
Through grave and hell, leading
Captivity captive
And now, onward He goes,
Adown the years, across the world
To live again the victory
Of glorious Calvary,
The show to men the overcoming power
With which He overcame
That it may be their own.

The Son of God

He loved me and gave Himself for me;
He loved me enough for Calvary;
All the joys above and His Father's love
He left for me.

He loved me and gave Himself for me,
As a man in the paths of Galilee;
From His humble birth, all His days on earth
Were spent for me.

He loved me and gave Himself for me;
All His body tortured to set me free;
And the cruel goad on the Roman road
Endured for me.

He loved me and gave Himself for me;
Through the hours of His Spirit's agony –
The sinner's death with His latest breath
He bore for me.

Consider Him

When in the fiery furnace tried
And when from everywhere are pressed
Trials, doubts and dangers –many a test –
Consider Christ the Crucified.

When storms come in on every side;
When icy winds of hate distress
And lashing rains of bitterness –
Consider Christ the Crucified.

When tempted to forsake the Guide
And grieve Him; when the flesh begins
To lead astray in secret sins –
Consider Christ the Crucified.

Consider Him, lest life should hide
That future glory set before
The Saviour, who our burden bore –
Consider Christ the Crucified.

Easter

And shall the earth renew again
        Her youth and yield her flowers?
Soon after winter's heavy rain
        Shall April bring her showers?
Through there is spring this Eastertide,
Shall it be so again, this side?

We shall See Him in the Morning

We shall see him in the morning
        when the mists of life have cleared,
with his arms outstretched to greet us
        from a journey we have feared.

Those who toiled all night and struggled
        till the earthly fight was won
will awaken to the music
        of his welcoming, "Well done!"

We shall recognise the Master
        with his wounded hands and side
as we worship him, the glorious,
        the ascended Crucified.

Though the shore now seems so distant
        we await the morning light
and the breakfast celebration
        when our faith gives way to sight.

For the Second Advent

Hail to You, by men despised,
      Sore ill-treated, crucified,
Now in Heaven, with God the Father
      Vindicated, glorified.
Hail our Lord at Your approaching
      At the appointed midnight hour,
Long awaited, long expected,
      Prince of peace and love and power.

Till to-day, a full salvation
      has been offered unto all,
Pardon, peace and joys unthought of,
      Gifts which with Your mercy fall
On the faithful, who repentant
      turn to You, as Christ the Lord,
Whom we hail at Your descending.
      Ever by our hearts adored.

Hail to You, our great Redeemer;
      Songs of everlasting praise
May we at Your second coming
      With one voice of gladness raise,
Joining with angelic anthems,
      New-found themes of holy joy;
All that now with sin is mingled
      Then to be without alloy.

Omnipresence

Beauty is urgent: like the cry
Of a child in the night;
Like the bell of an ambulance
Racing to avert
Death;
Like the roar of an aircraft
Falling to intercept
The foe.
Yet she is silent,
Like nightfall and the call
Of the Orient,
Voiceless as all
The world's great sorrows.
She is insistent
Like a cuckoo in May;
Distant
As Kanchinjinga,
Wrapped in her snows,
Always the background of the years,
Transient as life, yet
Immortal.

Lullaby For Christmas Eve

Sing me to sleep on Christmas Eve
      With a little lullaby
While the new moon and wintry stars
      Are lighting up the sky.
Sing me to sleep, sing me to sleep
While I am counting, counting sheep.

Rock me to sleep on this cold night
      When Jesus Christ was born;
I shall wake early I am sure,
      Before the Christmas dawn.
Rock me to sleep, rock me to sleep
While I am counting, counting sheep.

Sing me to sleep on this glad night;
      To-morrow will soon be here
Bringing a lovely Christmas Day,
      The best day of the year.
Sing me to sleep, sing me to sleep
While I am counting, counting sheep.

The River of Life

I

In Him was life, the light of men,
Life in Himself, as the Father had
In the millions of unmeasured years
When the morning stars were singing together
And the burning sun threw off a world.
In Him was life, by Him God made
Each universe and the Lord of life
Was light in the unknown yesterday.

When the earth was without her form and void
And darkness covered the face of the deep,
The Spirit of God moved over the waters,
And the chaos became the cosmos at length,
The unuttered Word of God was there
With God, in the fullness of time to come forth.

All things were made by Him and man,
The climax of creation, came
Into the world His hands had formed,
Into a world of blinding light
And many coloured depths of joy.

In Him was life, the essence of God,
Issuing forth on earth in men,
Made after the image of the Lord.
But God sent His life into the world
Transcendentally in Him,
The perfection of Divinity,
Through thirty years of human pain
And men beheld Him walk on earth,
The God-man bringing light and life.

While steadfastly the flame burned on,
A beacon in the world's dark night
Men saw it not, in blindness kept
By the decaying Jewish rites,
They understood not that He came
To bring them life, to manifest
The very heart of the Eternal.

In Him was life, gloriously
Shining in the darkness of human sin.

II

He came to His own, who received Him not;
Not those who ruled in the old religion,
In theory waiting for their King;
They said they had no King but Caesar.
Engrossed in ceremonial ways
And slaves to details of their cult,
They failed to see Messiah come,
The Word of God and the Life of God;
But still He came to the life of men,
In the midst of Roman rule He trod
To demonstrate in flesh and blood
The personality of God.

III

When His apprenticeship was over,
He came to Cana in Galilee,
Where the wine flowed freely for a while
And laughter and music lit the scene.
Jesus and His disciples were there,
Sharing in all the earthly joys

Of a marriage day. He came to life
At its merriest, sweetest, gayest time,
The very warp and woof of life,
To the hearts of men when their hearts were glad;
He came to change the water of grief
Into the wine of holy joy;
Such was His glory, to give, always
Plenty for want and life for death.

IV

There was a man who came by night
To see the Rabbi of the better Way,
By moonlit pathways of Jerusalem
To meet the Christ, to learn from Him
The deadness of the Jews religion
And the dire necessity of new birth;
Not reformation but regeneration,
Not forms and ceremony but new life,
Not entering into a mother's womb
But birth by Spirit and the Word of God
Through faith in Him, Who in the likeness
Of sinful flesh became the cure
Of that death-working force so like
The serpent in the wilderness.
Christ spoke to Nicodemus of the Jews
The leader of the Pharisees,
Striking at the roots of their formalism,
And the barrenness of the temple service,
Bringing spirit and liberty
From the cocoon of Judaism:
He that believeth in the Son hath life
But he that believeth not is dead.'

V

To the woman by the well side in Samaria,
Burdened with water and the load
Of her transgressions, he spoke in a figure
Of the resources in the deep, unfathomed well
That satisfies with its pure delight
The human heart. She came to draw
For needs that always must remain
In hers and every home, the need
For drink but Christ the great Physician
Soon diagnosed her deepest ill
And with unerring skill prescribed
The cure for heart and mind and will.

The spouse of many husbands, who
Lured men into her web with ease,
Some Cleopatra outliving grief,
Some Helen of the wars in Sychar,
Came to know the Saviour there,
The Bridegroom of the heart of man
The satisfier of the Soul, the Fount
Of life, whom knowing she forgot
Both water-pots and men and went
To tell of him in her city streets.

VI

For thirty-eight years he had known a death
By Bethesda's pool, eating and seeing,
Waiting for the moving of the water
In a dull monotony of life,

Until He came, life a thunder clap
Piercing the sultry atmosphere
Bringing wholeness of body and soul,
With a warning of a worse fate than impotence.
He brought new life, new hope, new horizons
In conquering the old infirmity,
And carrying away the vestiges of death,
One walked with Christ the new pathway
Of unrestricted life and passed
From death to life believing in Him.

VII

The Sower of the seed and the Lord of the harvest
Cut short His work on the mountainside,
Turned the poor best of a boy's resources
Into the plenty of His provision,
Feeding the thousands with enough and to spare
Out of the storehouses of His bounty
Out of the coffers of His grace;
He enriched the people by His power,
He satisfied their need for good
And sent them home to muse upon
The Bread of Heaven to earth come down,
To give His life for a dying world,
The necessary food of every man,
His daily bread, the Bread of life
Crushed, ground to powder in His death,
That man in eating His flesh should live,
For ever sustained by the life of God.

VIII

To the thirsting people in the temple courts,
He spoke the streams of living water
Flowing from Himself, the river of Life;
From the heart of the throne of God on high
Into the hearts of men, believing
In the Almighty's power; to flow
Onwards from the innermost being of man,
A constant supply of the waters of life.

IX

Whilst it was winter in Jerusalem
And winter in the hearts of His enemies,
He walked in the temple openly,
He spoke of His life laid down for men,
The shepherd laid down at the door of the sheep,
Across the sheepfold's entrance stretched;
He spoke of His care for the flock He bought
With His blood and of the eternal life
Which He would give to those who knew Him,
That they might never perish nor stray
From the keeping of the Father and from Him
The Eternal Son, the Saviour-Shepherd.

X

At His final entry into the City,
He faced the fiercest enemy,
He stood by the grave of Lazarus
With the sorrowing sisters of His friend.
The sceptics murmured, the Jews sympathised
Whilst Jesus wept and groaned in the spirit,

Remembering the havoc wrought by the foe,
And loving Lazarus and Mary and Martha,
Lifting His eyes to heaven He prayed
Standing on the world's dark battleground
Then into the fight with 'Lazarus,
Come Forth!' He spoke with compelling power
Of God Himself and he who was dead
Came forth, wearing the clothes of death
But manifesting essential life
In steps towards his family.
No wonder Christ could say beforehand
'I am the resurrection and the life,
He that believeth in Me, though dead,
Yet shall he live and living believers
Shall never die.' 'This Jesus shall die.'
Said Caiaphas, high priest for that year
And from that day man's fickleness turned
Darkly against the Lord of Life.

XI

Thomas, the doubter, called Didymus,
Listened to words of His Lord and God,
Who spoke of mansions beyond the world,
To which He soon must go to prepare
The fuller life for them. 'Whither
I go you know and the way you know.'
But Thomas did not understand,
And answered, 'How can we know the way?'
The Lord most patiently revealed
'I am the Way, the Truth and the Life,
No man may come to God except
By Me,' the Way into life's fullness.

XII

Christ went out to die, out into the night
Through the gardens of the Mount of Olives,
He spoke of the vine, lustrous on the temple –
The golden vine gleaned in the moonlight –
He spoke of Himself, in Whom was life
Coursing through His sacred veins,
The branches of the vine drawing
Their life from Him and bearing fruit;
He spoke of abiding, in simplicity,
Of resting assuredly in the life of God,
The Father, the patient Husbandman.

XIII

With eyes uplifted to heaven He cried
For the fast approaching hour of death
The hour of glory for the suffering Son,
Hanging on the cross of His atonement,
He spoke of eternal life in God,
So soon to glorify the Saviour,
That they might know the only true God
And Jesus Christ Whom He had sent.
In an earthly pilgrimage of thirty years,
He had finished the work He came to do
And so He passed, with the life of the ages
Reverberating in His spirit,
Calling to Himself men of the world
That they might know an endless life
In knowing God and Jesus Christ.

XIV

His conflict over and the cross
Emptied of death, He stood triumphant
On the day of resurrection, marked
With the wounds of His bitter crucifixion;
He stood in the garden in the early morning
Of the age of grace and life in the Son;
He had passed from the gloom of hell and death,
Passed through their gates and into the new
Unassailable life majestically.
Master and Lord and God, they called Him,
Possessor of powers they had never seen,
Released into perfection of life,
Unhindered now by the limits of time
And space, the Firstborn from the dead.

The Five Brothers

I

Bart.   I remember Dives with the highest regard;
      there was never a man who worked as hard.

Joseph   A fine example of an honest man;
      not a single flaw in the business he ran.

Nat.   For my part, I admired his family life
      and the way he looked after Rachel, his wife.

Simon   I'll join in these tributes to Dives our brother;
      did many good turns, to one and another.

James   As the youngest, perhaps I should sound a warning;
      he spoke to me in a dream, this morning.

II

Bart   Talk like that and you've got us all wincing
      and I guess we five would take some convincing.

Joseph   If he sends me a report from among the dead,
      it would pass, I am sure, right over my head.

Nat.   I know dear Dives wouldn't wish to alarm us
      or by devious means to disturb or harm us.

Simon   Come on then, James, what did he say;
      some gem to comfort us all on our way?

James   He begged that our values be completely changed,
      but the visit he hoped for could not be arranged.

Council Meeting

President Caiaphas
    takes his seat,
surveys the faces
    in smouldering heat,
Pharisee, Sadducee
    bent on defeat
        of the Son of God.

Tribal and family
    heads in a row,
ex-high priests
    in their dull after-glow,
legal advisers
    with an undertow
        of the Son of God

Nodding approval
    each traditionalist
of the old religion
    heartless formalist,
signals agreement
    to dispose of the Christ,
        this Son of God.

Not at the feast,
    they all agree
and the heavenly legions
    halt willingly
while the march of events
    points inexorably
        to the Lamb of God.

A Child's Death
(Remembering Julian and others)

Ask no questions. There are no answers
Silence follows the perfect days
lived out in the light of childhood,
unsullied by the arrogance,
the cynicism of age.

We grieve and you who nurtured him
have touched the depths of grief and loss
but, in that day when all is known,
you'll see his unspoiled youthfulness
as part of endless life.

Do they see everything at best
who only childhood know?

Footsteps

All the way to Calvary,
through Nazareth to Galilee,
Jerusalem and Jericho
Moscow, New York and Kabul
He came –and comes –unchangeably
to share in every tragedy.

A Vision –The Dawn of Salvation

I hold in vision the foster father
standing by the stable door,
uplifted hands to the morning sun
when, over the feeding trough as cradle
falls the shadow of a cross,
Joseph unknowingly enacting
the heart of man's salvation
in a single moment of time.

Harvest

We may not know the how and when
      of your unique creation
a universe of finitude
      and such divine perfection.

We join our hearts in thanks and praise
      for earth's right size and distance
from an all-powerful burning sun;
      for gravity's insistence.

Our moon as satellite of the earth
      gives tides and constant rhythm,
perfectly balancing land and sea
      in everlasting motion.

Mankind, the tenants of God's world,
      for care and maintenance,
sees the hand of the producer
      in His provenance.

Clay for bricks and timber for houses,
      leather from hides provided:
fine-grained rock releasing oil,
      in exploration guided.

These gifts of daily bread
      constantly keep us aware,
as we praise our changeless God
      for His amazing care.

In a Time of Change

The weathercock swings round,
    a centre of calm,
absorbing the gentlest breeze
    or the fiercest storm.

Nothing can add to or alter
    the pieces of truth
but a Hand will sometimes tap
    the kaleidoscope.

When spirits flag and hearts
    are numb and cold,
change comes as the angel
    of the changeless God.

January Sunset

Above the darkening pastel shades
of a January sunset,
    the slenderest moon
    hangs in celebration
ending a snowbound month.

Nor can the bleakest, blackest day
obscure the glory
    of another world
    seeking to affirm
a resurrection.

Always an evening star,
outshining the dusk,
    outlives the gloom
    and ruined hopes
of the Enlightenment.

For a Marriage Day

On this most beautiful of days
Our hearts unite in grateful praise
That You will cause our lives to bear
Some likeness to the Godhead here.

That, here united, maid and man
May share in Your creation's plan,
The love of God Incarnate show
Faintly reflected, here below.

May these, Your children, childlike be
In trust and true humility
And ever, with one heart and mind,
Your will in Christian service find.

Your light upon their pathway shed;
In darkness, may their steps be led
To know, in life's uncertainty,
The unknown ways Your eyes can see.

In a Day of Violence

Blood-stained and glorious time
When the infant church of Jesus Christ
Born of the aging Jewish faith
And cradled in the culture of the Greeks,
Grew to a healthy childhood.

'You are all Christians now', the Emperor said,
Declaring his allegiance officially
And thinking he could take over the growing church;
But his fickleness led him to alter course,
Blaming the Christians for the fire he started
And throwing them to the lions in the arena.

He played his fiddle while the city burned
And vice like a cancer gnawed at the heart
Of the once proud Empire which ruled the world.
Daubed with tar as human torches to light the
arena, those Christians died
In the full assurance of their faith.

Blood-stained and glorious time,
With Peter crucified upside down,
Reckoning himself unworthy of a similar
death to the Christ of God.
And Paul, who fought the good fight of faith,
Martyred at the gates of Imperial Rome.

Now only John of the Apostle survived
To speak and write immortally,
Living till the end of the first century.
Yet the church outlasted the Roman society
Where she was born, saving the men and women
Caught up in that doomed and crumbling world.

Blood-stained and glorious time
For Christians living under the threat
Of a savage death; no day for the waverers,
No time for a luke-warm kind of faith.
They met before daybreak on a working day,
On a Sunday, in the catacombs of Rome,
To remember, in symbols of bread and wine,
The Lord Whom they loved and followed to death.

Persecuted but not extinguished,
They spread their faith around the world
While Barbarians came down on the Empire at last
And Jerusalem itself went up in smoke;
They lived on in the seed of the martyr's blood
To carry the cross unashamedly on,
For Jesus to them was their peace and their Joy,
Their Leader, their Light, their Law and their God.

The Conversationalist

He can keep up ceaseless chatter
With well-worn patter on any subject.

He can cap any story with a better;
To every question he knows the answer.

He will not brook interruption;
In full spate, sweeps all before him.

He has been there or done it before you,
Possesses more of it than you and me.

He can turn any conversation but
Is not averse to completely ignoring.

Wait – with momentum of such high gearing
he may disappear in his vapourizing.

Jonah

In the unresting, watery waste,
      Abandoned by his foes,
Wave after wave passed over him
      And the dark tide rose.

There he trod untravelled ways
      Of green mystery;
Weeds entwined the prisoner,
      Locked within the sea.

Laid to rest in the restless deep,
      Alive, in the straits of death,
Monstrous jaws around him closed,
      Who breathed another's breath.

'In Letters of Hebrew, Latin and Greek'

On that barbaric altar,
     The Lord Christ died for me,
Victim of Jewish blindness
     And Roman apathy
Whilst Hellenistic culture
     Surveyed the tragedy.

Look down the nineteen hundred
     Years that have passed since then
And see the Christ – rejected
     By representative men –
Led out on each Good Friday
     To be crucified again.

One Star Differeth From Another Star In Glory

In clusters or in Milky Way,
     Orion or Pleaides,
We watch a glory journeying
     Down a million centuries.

Hands touch in frosty loneliness,
     Star reaches star in the night,
Whispering love in the wilderness,
     Borrowing and giving light.

Here with our little courses set
     Through warring constellations,
From soul to soul the splendours burn
     In a thousand generations.

When God
Became our Neighbour

('Whatever you did, for one of the least of these
brothers of mine, you did. for me'.

Matthew 24.40)

When God became our neighbour
in coming down to earth,
He took the name of Jesus
at His humble birth.
He always cared for others,
the lonely and the sad;
the helpless and the cripples
in meeting Him, were glad.

He told us that in seeking
for others in their need,
we give to Him devotion
in every loving deed.
So help us to be active
in coming to the aid
of those who will be feeling
most worried and afraid.

Release from fear and sadness
the house-bound and the old,
the prisoners of ageing
in our lives enfold;
and may the Lord's compassion
He comes to us to prove,
bind young and old together
in life-enriching love.

New-Town Church

1

The fields have given way, the trees are down,
New homes are here and work for everyone;
A people's life re-born in this new town,
Old industries transplanted, some begun.

And here amongst the shops and highways rise
The Concrete walls of a church making a start
With the new community; around her lies
A system needing a Christo-centric heart.

To the greater glory of God new talents bend
To build the fair with truth and with courage,
All sentimental clutter at an end,
Simplicity the key-note of the age.

There was a time when simple man could look
On coloured manuscripts of fresco style;
The stained-glass window was his picture book,
Which many a sermon-time did then beguile.

Now in the shrine with grace and dignity
Modern materials and methods mix
In this expression of Christian artistry,
Nothing that's mock or pseudo about the bricks.

II

The eastern aspect of the church
Speaking of the coming of Christ
Into the darkness of the world

And of his second coming when,
As lightning shining from the east,
He will in glory re-appear...
So build, for the rising of the Son,
Risen with healing in His wings,
Building with fine glass to welcome the light.

III

The rich men bring their thousands,
　　　　The poor men bring their pounds,
The artist brings a beauty
　　　　Breaking utility's bounds;
The architects and craftsmen
　　　　Have brought devoted skill
To foster the work and witness
　　　　Of the City set on a hill.

IV

In the days of gothic design, the churches
　　　　Caught the romantic, adventurous vision
And the Guilds of the City invaded poverty,
　　　　Fulfilling their Founder's self-giving mission.

For the church of that time was in the community
　　　　At the heart of its life. Bring back to the people
An active faith in adventure and giving,
　　　　Her influence no more remote as a steeple.

Once she refreshed the lonely traveller,
　　　　The church was his hostel for the night;
Here we must make room for the outcasts,
　　　　The misfits, the lonely, the bruised in the fight.

The Reformation builders expressed
　　　In the great City destroyed by fire
Through their rebuilding, revitalised spirit;
　　　Christopher Wren's glorious pulpit and spire.

V

Baptism were held in lake or stream
Or by the seaside, always publicly.
Then, with the coming of St Augustine,
Fervently teaching original sin,
Infants were baptised by the church
And in the first few centuries
The rite of confirmation came
With baptism of the professing Christian.
So in the glad acceptance of the faith
The Christian was washed, in a vivid picture,
Identified with Christ in death
And in triumphant resurrection,
Admitting thereby into the church
And blessing, in the laying on of hands
The new member of the body of Christ,
With a sign and a seal in the bonds of love.

O gift of human fellowship,
O gift of Father, Son and Spirit,
Blending the earthly with the heavenly:
So build within the temple courts
The font sunk at a lower level
For all to see the sacrament,
Whether in infants brought by their parents
Or adults in fullness of life and faith.

VI

Arrange the Holy Table at the Church's centre
Not out of sight as in medieval society,
For God has come with power into our time
And we must go from sheltered sanctuary,

Bearing a testimony in noisy street
Or crowded factory to the Christian Way,
Sustained and nourished by the Bread of Life
For the workaday world and the live-long day.

So sit around in Holy Communion
To receive the symbols of Sacrifice,
To eat the bread and drink the wine,
And remember redemption's bitter price.

VII

Forget the ruined bell-towers,
        The years have laid them waste,
Building the new spire of concrete
        And steel securely based;
The finger points us heavenward
        And leads us up and on,
Sounding the call to worship
        From the new carillon.

VIII

The angel-trumpets blow
Sounding in burning row,
The loud uplifted trumpets –
Gloria in Excelsis Deo.

The people sing in triumph,
Voices, cymbals and strings
Blend in the Church's worship
Borne on the organ's wings.

Come to the dedication;
Full-throated harmony
Praising Him in the choir
With flute-stop delicacy.

IX

Rise up, O men, and build
    In the streams of unfouled air,
While time remains to rescue
    From the orgies of despair.

The Babel towers are painted
    In colours of prosperity
But the weapons of war are ready
    And peace is illusory.

Rise up and build the city
    The Master Builder is *God*,
Already within her precincts
    Millions of feet have trod.

The Still Sad Music

'Lord You Have Known'

Lord, you have known my downsitting
And my uprising – the come and go
Of life's long littleness,
The moments of departure and arrival,
Waking and lapsing into unconsciousness,
Setting out for the market place
Or back from the fields;
To the longest working day
You saw me go.

You noticed me and knew about
The unimportant times (as I thought of them),
You loved me all the way
As I returned from the far country,
From the land of no-pasture
Back to an inheritance;
Through unseen watchfulness,
When human love forgot,
You welcomed me.

Working Through Disappointments

Lord God, you know they seemed so great,
those many disappointments and frustrations
        which I met when hopes were high
        but now I see them as just part
of a detailed plan for me.

I cannot tell what tomorrow holds
of joy and laughter, pain and tears
        but offer thanks for what is past
        and when some things come back to haunt
I clasp the hand of One who knows the way.

The Pilgrim's Progress

With the passing of the years,
With the slackening of fires,
With the quietening of fears,
    Comes a special peace.

Through the thickest of the fight,
Through the lifting of a weight,
Through the ending of the night,
    Grows an inward calm.

Whilst the thunder clap my peal,
Whilst the restless waves still roll,
Whilst the hurt still leaves its weal,
    There is more certainty.

By that Presence shadowing,
By an Influence unseen,
By a Grace of which I sing,
    We shall overcome.

Standing Committees

They seldom stand for long
Or for much,
Leastways for propositions
On which they sit
Indefinitely.

They often shoot the bull,
Then pass the buck,
Sign three copies and sit
On their tails. They take minutes
And waste years.

'Out of the Depths'

Lord, I believe you. Help with my unbelief,
For I believe in your deep love and mercy,
In your forgiving understanding
Of the human heart.
       Through lonely watches of the spirit's night
       Within the narrow tunnel of my grief,
          I know a quiet dawn will come.
       Tortured alone in the creeping, loathsome dark
       And dragged along a labyrinthine maze,
          I still believe your healing sun
       Will bring the birth of some new day
       To break the iron gates of pain,
To bring, again, life where hopes, broken, lie
Crippled among her ancient battlements;
Lord, I believe that there will surely be
Light, after the midnight burns to death.

Photo-Finish

A Baptist, a Brother, an Anglican
       Arrived on the heavenly scene,
Delighted to find that their differences
       Were not what they once had been;
Old battles about bishops and deacons,
       Immersion and sprinkling were done
For the Baptist, the Brother, the Anglican
       In a photo-finish, had *all* won.

A Name

How clearly a name chimes down the years
From the ruined bell-towers of the past,
Echoing through the cloisters of memory,
Unforgettably reverberating, deathlessly calling.

They who were yesterday triumphant,
Weaving their bright aureoles,
Glow with a lustre still, as Napoleon,
But only a name remains, endlessly crying.

Faces pass and their laughter with them;
Features change; heroes and lovers must die,
While a name rides on into the eternal
Life of the future, its own praise or threnody.

Death Of An Indian Summer

Standing back, we watched the hillside,
Daubed with gold and brown,
Where an overdue Indian summer
Overtook climbers and motorists
Lingering in the warmth
In shirt-sleeves and cotton dresses.

Two weeks later rain mingled with gold dust
Falling from silver birches
And glinting in pale sunlight,
I pulled back the yellow cloth
With a shoe's sideways sweep,
Heaping leaves at the burial of summer.

The Unbroken Heart

John Crick, he married Janet
    When he was forty-three;
Of all the girls in Tooting
    The plainest maid was she.

But Janet served him truly
    With wifely modesty;
'A very sound investment'
    Thought John, 'for the likes of me.'

Jim Scott was wed at twenty
    To Jane in Buckhurst Hill,
Their love was brave and shining
    Like the early daffodil.

They had three children quickly
    But life grew sad and plain
And the storms were fierce and sudden
    In the hearts of Jim and Jane.

John Crick, across the gardens,
    Condemned them out of hand;
'Just how these people manage,
    I do not understand.'

But John still cherished Janet;
    At least, he thought he did,
While the gentle art of living
    From his blind heart was hid.

He took a pride in marriage,
　　　　(He did in gardening);
When Janet died one winter,
　　　　He said, 'Now there's a thing.

I thought I'd backed a winner,
　　　　Quite young and healthy she,
To leave me at this moment,
　　　　It's one ... big ... mystery.'

Old Couples on Trains

Not much to say – all has been said
and said a thousand times before.
　　　　They quietly pass the hours, in thought
　　　　recalling other railway trips
made in leisurely days of steam.

The landscape is still green, the corn
is ripe, farmhouses almost unchanged,
　　　　more cars in car parks everywhere,
　　　　high flats in country towns, these things
must go unsaid on the Inter-City train.

Remembering how young people travel
across the world by more exciting means,
　　　　they wonder where it all will end,
　　　　as minds fall back through fifty years
to joys on the London, Brighton, South Coast line.

For Sale

Death's slow paralysis
Over him stole,
Ashen-grey, bent
In body and soul.

His house, like his frame,
Quite empty lies;
Vanished the light
From windows and eyes.

The creeper is black
On the stucco wall
And the Holland blinds
Allowed to fall.

To the shrivelled past
Of life's history
He hastened, there,
Dying to be,

Joining the glories,
He was loath to forsake
Whilst of his detached villa
Two flats they will make.

On Listening to Sir Watford Davies's 'Solemn Melody'

On a morning as ageless as the sea
And timeless as springtime in Arcady,
They walked, I saw in slow procession
Down some Whitehall or Piccadilly,
Alive again in the eternal present
Of Hanover or Stuart where
Death walked no more to separate
A king or queen from a natural heir.
Plantagenets and Tudors met
In the gay sunlight, as monarchy
Crowded in the avenue of time
And stored at the gates of history.
Defeated, victorious, grave or uncouth,
Obstinate, sightless, brave, they came,
Cheered or hated, mourned or forgotten
The silent, the merry, the dashing, the lame;
Henrys and Edwards, Richards and Alfred
Elizabeth, Stephen, Mary and Anne,
Immortal, yet passing across the stage,
Unchanged in the age of the Common Man.

The Twelve Months of Man

Like January is the infant -
    Until he is six –
Snowdrops and the snow
    In innocency mix.

Childhood takes us to February,
    The next six years
Like the anguish of the earth,
    The pain and the tears.

March with her youthfulness
    Brings us to eighteen,
With the first of life's flowers,
    The gold and the green.

Then, in the flood-tide of spring
    To twenty-four
With April as the lover,
    Manhood at the door.

May, with her blossoms
    At thirty years;
Whisperings of high summer,
    The hopes and the fears.

Follow the long days of June,
    The height of the story;
Midsummer days of man
    And the hours of his glory.

From then till forty-two
    The broad fields lie,
Flooded with the settled light
    Of a hot July

The next six years are sultry;
    Grown dull, we tire
In the heat of August days
    And the slackened fire.

With shortened breath and step
    At fifty-four,
We stoop in many fields
    Gleaning our store.

At sixty in October,
    The leaves come down;
The chill wind of autumn
    Makes older men frown.

The year is in retirement,
    The days are sear
And sight is dim and misty
    When November's here.

Now we are in December,
    Three score and ten;
Life's end, unless our infancy
    Come round again.

Written at 20,000 ft.

Fortunately for the future of that shrinking world,
travel is no longer only for the rich or clever –
the young move freely now through every continent.

They swarm across the glossy transit lounges
with next to nothing in the way of clothes,
eager to fly wherever and at no small cost;

to work or not to work, relaxed, foot loose and free,
their assets so majestically themselves, but plus
and often crumpled, treasured, passport for the world.

Keepsake

This is a prayer I must not pray –
That on some glorious, autumn day
          You'll care for me

Mrs Curwen

Very frail is Mrs Curwen
But she rules her home with zest;
Local shops, respecting wisdom,
Only send their sparkling best.

Very sad is Mrs Curwen
Speaking of her younger son;
At his wedding she reflected
How his troubles had begun.

Very shrewd is Mrs Curwen
Dealing with her other boy;
Cheaply she provides more comfort
Then most married men enjoy.

But so old is Mrs Curwen
That her Basil will be free
Soon to bring an Indian summer
To their ancient family tree.

He Never Married

Settled in aspic lie
The biographical facts
Of obituary notice.

Pointless to ask the question
Seeing he cannot reply
And other answers are suspect.

He kept his secret to the grave:
No-one will ever know for
He remained, more than most, an enigma.

They said he had numerous friends,
Hinted darkly at a girl who died
And mentioned the Oedipus complex.

One even swore he was married
And lived apart from his wife
Whom no-one had ever seen.

Some blamed his absorbing work,
Said he preferred freedom to marriage,
(he was not the marrying kind).

He was too fussy, too mean, they said.
He had said it unfair for a girl
To marry a middle-aged man.

So now we will never know
And he often asked himself,
'I wonder why I am single.'

Cotswold Idyll

Not hills in any real sense,
Cotswolds gently undulate,
dry-stone walls, limestone houses
with age hardening to gold.

Windrush's clear, bright stream
flowing through Bourton-on-the-Water
near Risingtons, Great, Little and Wyck
past Slaughters, Lower and Upper.

Stow-in-the-Wold at the centre,
Nortons, Chipping and Over,
Evenlode quietly passing
Edward Thomas's Adelstrop.

Northward to Moreton-in-Marsh
where once four counties met –
Gloucestershire, Worcestershire,
Warwickshire and Oxfordshire.

Fairford, Bibury and Burford,
Northleach and north to Broadway
with Campdens, Chipping and Broad –
a canvas of England's heart.

Triplets

Unremarkable except as triplets,
they had a normal childhood,
doing their different things
          at home, at school.

One became a famous artist,
another ran a business,
the third became an Olympic
          gold medallist.

In later years, losing touch,
one day they decided to meet,
despite the crowds, in London
          at Victoria Station.

With no arrangements made on dress,
they were amused to find
they wore completely
          identical clothes.

The Poet Laureate

Others excluded themselves
          without exception,
so the Motion was carried
          with no objection.

Lodge Meeting

He drove his cab through London streets,
a very poor day, no one about,
so he was looking forward to lunch
at the Lodge Meeting near his home.

'Won't cost me much, twenty quid,
to go to Charities; one day I'll go
through the chair but to-day I'll leave
before the real proceedings start.

Others will be sent out before me;
can't think why they come except,
like me, their turn will come one day.
Oh forget the cab, I'm on my way.'

Eight Months' Winter
(i.m. R.S. Thomas)

We celebrate – you would hate that –
your devotion to unfriendly soil,
your flock scratching a rock-hard living,
you ministering to the doubts and fears
of Dai Puw, Llew Puw and Huw Puw,
Evans and Iago Prytherch.

You could find God in a chainsaw,
yet everywhere challenges to faith
among the lonely hill farmers where
you wove your own religious odyssey,
austere and unyielding
around a tall and empty cross.

Blue Whales

For fifty million years
you flourished in the unknown
     world of water,
singing your mating songs
across the ocean beds
     through thousands of miles.

Once, explosive harpoons
tried to eliminate
     our largest creature
but now, in Californian seas,
you feed and frolic in lives
     of pastime and passion.

By the Pool

Menus are standing,
Chairs empty;
Children come noisily
to the heated pool
but the hotel cries out
for extra trade
from occupied seats
and obese men.

Finding a Comet

A spacecraft searches
in galaxy after galaxy
for a comet formed
four million years ago.

Unimaginable in speed,
it lands eventually
on a surface of ice and dust,
glorious in frailty,

Infinity in the universe,
reflecting the infinity
of a creator, leaves us
not knowing the unknowable

Looking Over Ashdown Forest

From here we overlook
a forest in its glory,
deciduous, coniferous,
leaf with leaf inspiring.

Smoke rising from the centre
tells of life within,
arduous, various,
lonely, welcoming.

Towns in all directions,
flourish as outcrop,
famous, virtuous,
centres of becoming.

My Country

My country, I always think of you
      with all your blemishes and pains;
but in millions of children's faces,
      tumbles and laughter, beauty remains.

The homes of the brave, the fearful, the old
      in villages, towns and cities
tell us the story of life to the full,
      lived out with its pleasures and pities.

The woodland, lakeside, mountain and street
      bind us together with infinite care:
in riches and poverty, sickness and health
      we mix through foul weather and fair.

This is a land of people so great,
      surviving the onslaught of war;
we take heart in thankfulness, journeying on
      where millions have stepped out before.

That path of our fathers still remains,
      guiding and strengthening faltering ways
to bring back and lead on to better things
      and offer continuing praise.

A Song of England

There are no fields like those that lie
　　Under an English heaven;
Russet and brown, golden and green,
　　From Oxford to the Severn.

There are no hills like those that roll
　　Bare-backed down to the sea,
Cradling the Sussex villages
　　From Firle to Chanctonbury.

There are no trees like those that stand
　　Firmly in Norman shires;
Oak, elm and ash and beech below
　　The tallest poplar spires.

There were no men like those that died
　　For freedom and her sons;
Edmund and Harold and Hereward –
　　The story of England runs.

These are the fields and hills they knew
　　Who fell before the foe,
Gave to the countryside its peace
　　A thousand years ago.

Nakedness

(The nakedness of woman is the work of God.
William Blake.)

It was no accident,
the peak of creation,
designer work
to perfection.

Man needed the incentive
to ensure the future
of himself through another
living creature.

No wonder the system
gives great pleasure
but sometimes confusion
without measure.

Single Parent

Young and beautiful,
she gave him love –
nothing more –
through childhood
and teenage years.
He does not look back
or on with anxiety;
his constant security
is all he knows.

Biographical

Born in 1912 and educated at two small private schools in South London, Randle Manwaring spent all his working life in the Insurance Industry, becoming a Managing Director of a Lloyd's firm of Insurance Brokers in the course of which he did a year as President of the Society of Pension Consultants.

After leaving the City, Randle did a Master's degree in history at Keele University and, more recently, was awarded a doctorate in hymnody by Mellen University in the U.S.A.

In the war years, he served in the RAF, was one of the founding officers of the RAF Regiment, responsible for the whole of their operation in Burma and for taking the swords from defeated Japanese generals at a ceremony in Rangoon.

He has served on various poetry society committees, done reviews and taught poetry for a brief while to dyslexic children.

There have been a good number of anthology appearances but perhaps the most interesting was when Professor Shotaro Oshima of Waseda University in Japan included one of Randle Manwaring's poems in his book "How To Read an English Poem."

Also by Randle Manwaring

PROSE

The Heart of this People (Quaintance)	(1954)
A Christian Guide to Daily Work (Hodder)	(1963)
The Run of the Downs (Caldra House)	(1984)
** From Controversy to Co-existence (C.U.P)	(1985)
The Good Fight (Howard Baker Press)	(1990)
** A Study of Hymn-writing and Hymn-singing in the Christian Church (Edwin Mellen Press)	(1991)
Songs of the Spirit in Poetry and Hymnody (Mellen)	(2004)
On the road to Mandalay (Pen & Sword)	(2006)

POETRY

Posies Once Mine (Fortune Press)	(1951)
Satires and Salvation (Mitre Press)	(1960)
Under the Magnolia Tree (Outposts)	(1965)
Slave to No Sect (Mitre Press)	(1966)
* Crossroads of the Year (White Lion)	(1975)

* From the Four Winds (White Lion)   (1976)

In a Time of Unbelief (Henry Walter)   (1977)

* Thank You, Lord Jesus (Henry Walter)   (1980)

The Swifts of Maggiore (Fuller d'Arch Smith)   (1981)

In a Time of Change (Coventry Lanchester Polytechnic) (1983)

Collected Poems (Charles Skilton)   (1986)

Some Late Lark Singing (Brentham Press)   (1992)

Love so Amazing (Ikon)   (1995)

Trade Winds (Palancar)   (2001)

Poems of the Spirit (Mellen)   (2004)

*   For children
**   Also second editions